# WATERCOLOR

## STYLES AND TECHNIQUES

This edition published in 2017
By SpiceBox™
12171 Horseshoe Way
Richmond, BC
Canada V7A 4V4

First published in 2010
Copyright © SpiceBox™ 2010

ISBN 10:   1-77132-014-1
ISBN 13:   978-1-77132-014-6

CEO and Publisher: Ben Lotfi
Editorial: AnnMarie MacKinnon
Creative Director: Garett Chan
Art Director: Christine Covert
Design & Layout: Leslie Irvine & Kirsten Reddecopp
Production: James Badger, Mell D'Clute
Sourcing: Janny Lam, Jin Xiong

For more SpiceBox products and information, visit our website:
www.spiceboxbooks.com

Manufactured in China

7 9 10 8

# CONTENTS

# INTRODUCTION

Watercolors are quite possibly the oldest paint medium in existence—prehistoric cave paintings were essentially done in watercolors—but they are by no means old fashioned. In fact, then, as now, watercolors are extremely versatile. They allow the painter to achieve a wide variety of looks with just a few simple adjustments of pigment to water ratios. They're easy to transport and are a wonderful medium with which to experiment with outdoor painting. Also, because they're water-based, they're easy to clean.

As you go through the book, you'll learn sketching and painting techniques that will help you translate the world you see around you into your art. You'll have the opportunity to explore different ways of seeing your surroundings. You'll explore light and composition in a way that you perhaps have not done before. As you become more familiar with watercolors and their possibilities, you'll begin to experiment and learn new ways to handle this exciting medium.

# CHOOSING THE RIGHT PAPER

Paper grade and texture will have an effect on your work. Smooth paper allows the paint to go on flat (left), whereas a rougher paper will tend to break up the paint (right), creating an attractive texture.

## Scaling up a drawing

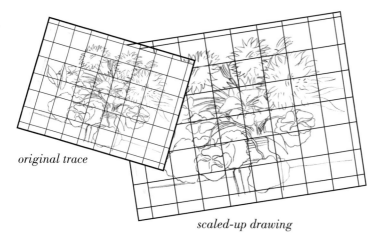

*original trace*

*scaled-up drawing*

To copy a complex composition, trace it, and draw a regular grid over it. Then enlarge the grid proportionally onto the size sheet you desire and transfer the sketch, square by square, onto the larger sheet.

# SIZING YOUR PAPER

Because you are painting with very watery paint, you must treat your paper first, otherwise it will buckle and form troughs in which paint will puddle and ruin your work.

First use a sponge to wet your paper all over with clear water. Fix it with masking tape to a rigid board and let it dry totally before starting to paint.

The paper will stay flat and smooth, and the tape will act as a border while you paint. You can tilt the board to ease the flow of paint over the paper, creating attractive runs when working wet into wet.

# USING COLOR

An understanding of color and how it is formed
is the first step to creating beautiful paintings.

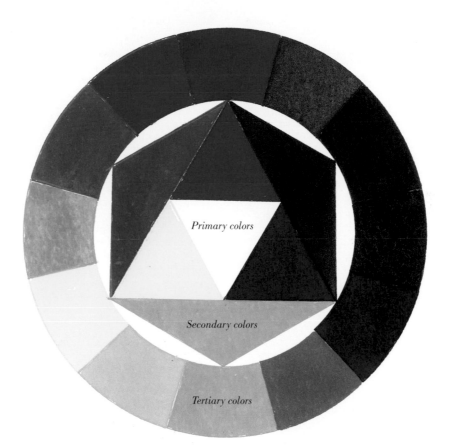

*Primary colors*

*Secondary colors*

*Tertiary colors*

**The color wheel**

The color wheel is the best way to visualize
how colors are mixed and the way they relate
to each other.

**Primary colors**—yellow, red, blue—are
the colors from which all others are made.

**Secondary colors**—orange, violet, green—
are mixed from equal parts of two primaries.

**Tertiary colors** are made by mixing equal
parts of a primary color and the secondary
color nearest to it.

# COMPLEMENTARY COLORS

Any color's complementary is the one
exactly opposite it on the color wheel.
To produce a primary color's
complementary, just mix the other two
primary colors, as shown here. When
used together, complementary colors
"bounce off" each other and create
a feeling of energy. The pairing of
opposites—such as a bluish green and a
deep orange—can be much more subtle,
but no less effective, than these examples
of primary and secondary colors.

# LIGHTENING AND DARKENING COLORS

Adding water to a color is the best way to lighten it, producing a "thin"—as opposed to a "strong"—mix. Adding white will make the paint opaque but is good when you want to add highlights at a late stage.

Surprisingly, you do not need black when trying to get a dark color. You can create dark tones by adding blues, reds, browns, greens, or oranges. Adding the complementary produces a lively color, while adding black tends to deaden it.

*with water*

*with white*

*with black*

*with orange*

## *Helpful Hint*

Be careful when mixing that you keep your color combinations simple and fresh—try not to muddy them by overmixing or adding too many colors.

*with water*

*with white*

*with black*

*with green*

# COLOR TINT CHART

Group your colors in the way shown. Paint a strong tone of the color in the first of the three boxes then make a medium tone made by adding a little white paint, then a light tone by adding even more white. This will show you the color and two of its lighter shades.

+White ++White

Cadmium Red

+White ++White

Alizarin Crimson

+White ++White

Ultramarine Blue

+White ++White

Cerulean Blue

+White ++White

Prussian Blue

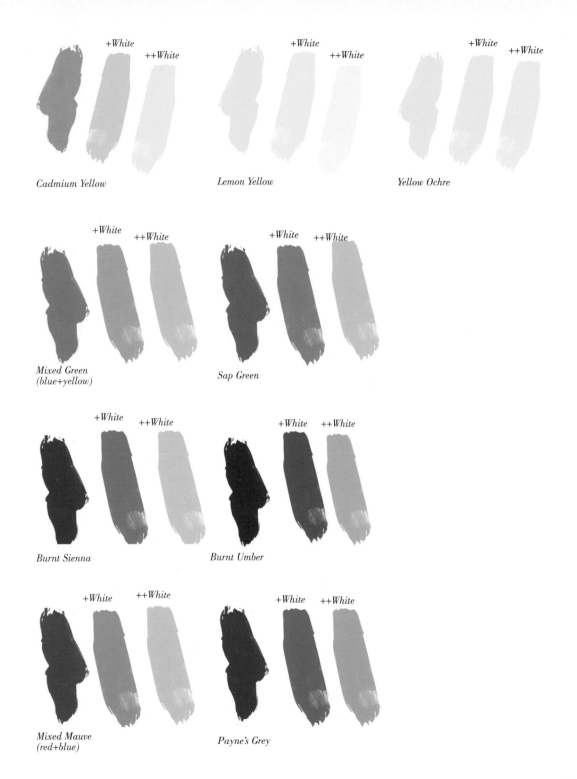

+White    ++White

Cadmium Yellow

+White    ++White

Lemon Yellow

+White    ++White

Yellow Ochre

+White    ++White

Mixed Green
(blue+yellow)

+White    ++White

Sap Green

+White    ++White

Burnt Sienna

+White    ++White

Burnt Umber

+White    ++White

Mixed Mauve
(red+blue)

+White    ++White

Payne's Grey

Here is a good example of how subtle combinations of colors have produced the wide range of dark and light tones used for shadows and highlights. The colors are not completely mixed before they are applied, giving a pleasing variation that adds dynamism to the painting.

# MIXING COLOR ON THE PAGE

There are essentially two ways of mixing colors: on the palette, and on the page.

Mixing on the palette may seem the more straightforward way, but because watercolor is a transparent medium, mixing colors on the page, in the process of painting, can offer some wonderful creative possibilities.

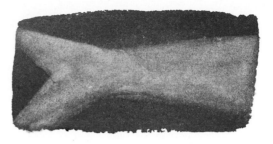

Here are three of the most popular "mixing" techniques. Top: painting wet into wet blurs colors together. Left: making glazes with wet on dry washes creates subtle combinations. And below: the dry brush technique produces lively looking broken color on the surface of the paper.

## Mixing color on the palette

Avoid making flat, homogeneous mixes on your palette. Instead, pick up paint on the brush a little at a time, in various combinations, keeping many different mixes going at the same time. This produces a much more pleasing result.

Keep scraps of paper next to your work so you can experiment with mixes before using them. If mixes dry out, rewet with a little water, but at the end of a painting session clean your palette.

# FLAT WASH

Making a wash of diluted paint is the most basic skill in watercolor. It is called "flat" because it produces a continuous, even finish.

To wash a large area, take a brush of premixed watery color and make a long stroke across the top of the paper. Work down the sheet in this way in alternating directions, picking up the bottom edge of the previous stroke and tilting the board so that paint runs down slightly. Mix enough paint for the whole area, and work fast.

*Helpful Hint*
Apply washes with a smooth, continuous stroke. Do not lift your brush or go over your work or the flat tone will be disturbed.

**1** A series of flat washes allows you to build up progressive tones of color, in this case to depict the darkening colors of the mountains the nearer they are to the viewer. Begin by laying down a flat wash for the sky.

**2** Now paint the most distant mountains with a pale wash of color, increasing the depth of tone by adding more blue to the mix as you work toward the closest mountains. Ensure that there is only a small tonal difference between successive colors, and that each wash is dry before you apply the next one.

*Note that a "wash" does not have to cover a large area—it is simply a term for flowing color onto paper, however small the space.*

As you can see, it is possible to create subtle gradations of tone using only flat washes.

Another way to get variation is to gradually add water or introduce additional colors into a wash as you work down the paper; this is known as a "graded wash."

# WET ON DRY

Laying down a new wash over another one that has already dried is an excellent way to build up color.

Because watercolor is a transparent medium, it can be difficult to get really intense colors. But by laying down a series of washes, one on top of the last—a technique called "glazing"—it is possible to get great depth and subtlety.

Painting wet on dry is also an effective way of mixing colors on the paper, as one wash is visible through the next: crimson over violet gives a rich red, sienna over pink creates a deep coppery color, and so on. You can paint light tones over dark or dark over light.

See how this cherry is built up, layer by layer. The first pale wash delineates shape and marks out the highlight. The next begins to give form and contour. Then subsequent washes refine contours and add depth of tone and color, creating a realistic object that positively glows with life.

## Helpful Hint
For the richest tones and greatest impact, apply dark tones over light; light paint over dark will produce a milky, hazy effect.

# FRUITY STILL LIFE

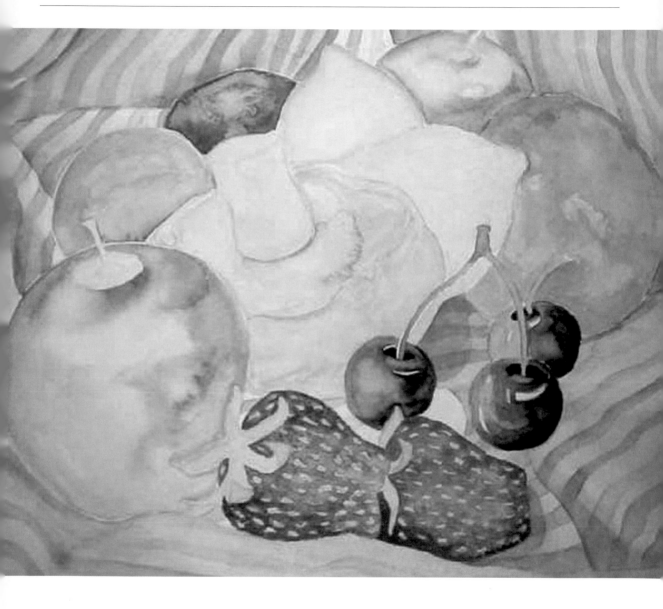

**1** Put in your palest washes first, then let your painting dry. Some colors are more transparent than others when thinned with water, so it is best to experiment with test swatches on a scrap of paper. White paint is usually opaque, so do not use it to lighten transparent washes. Get pale tones by adding water instead.

## Helpful Hint

If you blow on your paper to speed the drying process, do not blow too hard on very wet paint or you may spread it all over the paper.

**2** You can build up the whole painting, layer by layer, or you may prefer to work on one section at a time, completing it before moving on to another. As you are working, consider where you will place shadows and highlights.

Remember that your washes don't have to be flat—you may want to add colors wet into wet to get a mottled effect. And you can always add some dry brush details or highlights at the end.

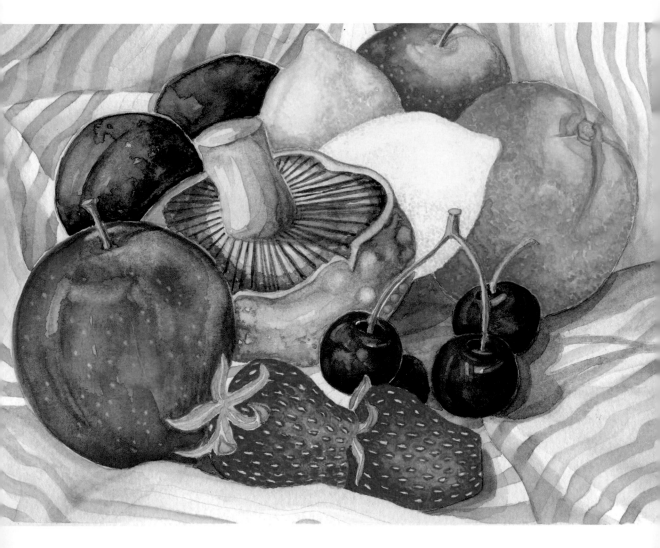

# WET INTO WET

Painting wet into wet is what gives watercolor its unique characteristic—a delicate, flowing, luminous quality unmatched by any other medium.

Watercolor will run and blur when it hits wet paper, and you can exploit this tendency to great effect.

When used in a free-flowing manner, wet into wet is often combined with masking fluid to protect light areas.

Here, masking fluid was painted over the shapes of lizards and a greenish wash laid down. Wet, darker colors were dropped in, forming loose shapes and colors. When the masking fluid was rubbed off, another yellow wash was run over the area, disturbing the previous wash and picking up some of the color—all contriving to produce a watery scene.

*See Using Masking Fluid, page 45.*

Wet into wet can be used in a more controlled manner. Paint an area or figure in a pale tint, then go over with another color while still wet to create soft forms and shadows.

You can also lift out spots of wet washes with a sponge to create highlights—or to blot out and correct areas where the paint has run too freely.

*Helpful Hint*
Dry paper can be lightly rewetted so that new color dropped in will merge and blend with the wash already laid down.

# SEAFOOD PLATTER

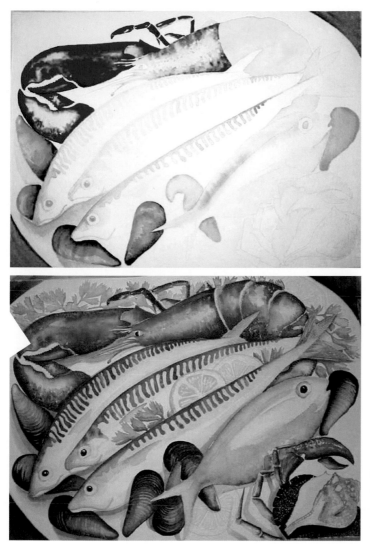

**1** Work wet into wet on one section or object at a time. Start by loading your brush with the palest of washes and covering the area.

**2** Continue to build up color and definition, one section at a time, by wetting an area and stroking in another wash.

**3** On a painting as complex as this, be prepared to work slowly and to build up layers of washes. Occasionally add a stroke of water to blur an edge or to lighten a tone.

Even with a buildup of washes, the painting retains a translucent quality, thanks to the wet-into-wet technique.

Add final details by painting wet on dry.

# DRY BRUSH

The combination of dry pigment and the textured surface of the paper produces a grainy, "broken" stroke. Dry brush can be worked over painted or unpainted paper with any brush—thick, thin, pointed, or flat—as long as both the brush and the paper are dry. Be careful to use the right amount of paint: too much will produce a muddled effect and too little will not give ample coverage.

This technique is useful for reflections and highlights, and for depicting natural phenomena, including wispy clouds, shimmering foliage, sparkling snow, and fast-flowing water. Its dynamic quality often expresses movement.

*Fish scales*

*Rough bark*

Use a dry brush to represent many effects found in nature. See how you are able to combine colors in a subtle way, and to use the visible direction of the brush stroke to define motion and contour.

*Animal fur or hair*

*Blowing grasses*

You can also use the dry brush technique over a flat wash to give it character and definition.

# LIZARDS ON SAND

**1** Using your broad brush loaded with wet paint, make a wash over the page and let it dry. Here, the figures have been masked off to resist the wash.

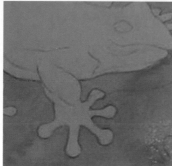

**2** To make your texture, your brush should be starved of water before lifting pigment from the palette. Drag it over the surface.

## Helpful Hint

For the most pleasing results, use toning colors for your top and bottom layers—either light over dark, or dark over light.

**3** Whatever figures you paint will be enhanced by such an interesting background. In this case, its parched, sandlike quality complements the glistening bodies of the lizards.

In general, textured strokes such as dry brush are best in combination with other techniques such as flat washes so that the effect does not become overwhelming.

# CREATING TEXTURES

## Sponging

Sponging paint—on or off— is an excellent way of creating a mottled surface. Use a fairly dry sponge dipped in color and dab it onto the surface of wet or dry paper. You can sponge dark over light, or vice versa.

Alternatively, use a clean, damp sponge to lift the paint off, creating a smoother, lightened effect.

*See also Lifting Out, page 32.*

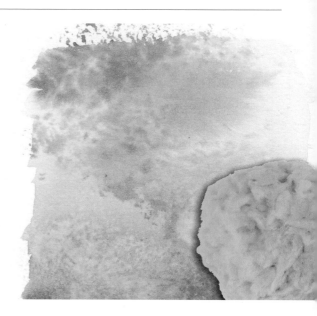

## Scumbling

Scumbling is a "scrubbing" action used to create a loose texture that is effective for depicting foliage. Use a fairly stiff dry brush loaded with thick paint—either wet or dry—and apply onto a dry background, in a light, rhythmic, circular motion.

## Stippling

Stippling creates a texture similar to pointillism. It is done with the end of a stiff, flat dry brush containing a small amount of paint.

Apply with a quick, light dabbing motion, possibly over a stencil to control shapes. To create shadow and form, apply successive layers of color to dry paper, and let parts of the underlayers show through. Do not work wet or let colors merge.

## Spattering

Spatter paint from a toothbrush loaded with color. With the brush facing down, close to the paper, draw your thumb along the bristles toward you. The fine spray gives a "loose" look and has many uses— from soft shadows to flowers in a meadow.

## Scratching out

Form highlights by removing paint from the paper's surface.

Paint your image, then while the paper is still wet, use the slanted tip of your brush handle (or the edge of a plastic card) to scratch out broad highlights where required. You need to press down fairly hard to displace the color.

You can create a similar effect by carefully scratching off dry paint using a sharp craft knife. Because it damages the paper, it is best to limit this to small areas.

## Lifting out

If you want a more subtle, even ghostly effect, lift off wet paint with a brush or sponge.

Instead of scratching away wet color to reveal highlights, you can use a damp brush to lift the color away, creating pale areas and shapes. You can also blot the area you have just dampened with a sponge to leave soft blurred lines.

Lift out when your initial background washes are about half-dry.

*See also Sponging, page 29.*

# PAINTING WATER

Painting wet into wet is the most popular technique for depicting water.

Calm water: Lay down a pale wash, then stroke darker colors into it. Usually, water gets lighter as it meets the horizon, so let your strokes become darker nearer the foreground. Tilt your painting board slightly so that the dark colors run downward.

Choppy water: Apply paint in curved strokes, letting them blend into each other, with white paper showing between the strokes to simulate light bouncing off the surface of the water.

Loose waves make larger brush strokes.

Create froth by letting paper show through within the stroke and by allowing paint to drip vertically in places. Stroke in darker paint at the top of the waves.

Reflections: Create them in a previously laid wash by rewetting it and then making narrow horizontal strokes below the object to be reflected, in a suitable color. Tilt your board slightly to let your strokes blend together vertically. Reflections can also be worked in a more controlled way, creating a regular pattern.

# COLD MOUNTAIN LAKE

**1** First lay down your background wash for the water. When this is dry, use a small round brush to add choppy, slightly curved strokes. In the foreground use a large round brush to apply longer, thicker, and darker strokes.

At the bottom of the painting, the brush strokes hold less liquid paint and have become dry looking. This creates an illusion of light shimmering on the surface.

**2** For added interest, use the dry brush technique to add grasses in the foreground once the paper has completely dried.

# PAINTING CLOUDS

With just a few carefully observed brush strokes, you can conjure up clouds of every mood and description.

The first thing to notice about clouds is that they are not flat; they are three-dimensional and show light and shadow. They also contain color.

Try a sunny sky first. Paint the blue patches between the clouds and, when these are dry, paint the clouds' shadowy undersides.

For hazier areas, work wet into wet. Dampen the paper and lay down a few horizontal strokes of color. Then tilt the paper to let the colors run into each other and blur.

Soft edges: Where you want clouds with very soft edges, dampen that area and then paint the sky so it blurs into the clouds.

Lightened areas: To soften more edges or lighten any area that seems too dark, scrub with a wet bristle brush and pick up the loose color with a sponge.

Darkened areas: In other places, drop in unmixed dark colors to provide dramatic contrasts.

# THREATENING CLOUDS

Create the feeling of storm clouds by using more subdued colors and deeper shadows. Horizontal strokes of this same tone can also be used along the horizon to cast a menacing gloom and suggest bleak distance.

Use clear water on your brush to blur the edges of some of the clouds and to show faint light filtering through.

## *Helpful Hint*
Not all clouds are painted wet into wet. Use white on a dry brush to stroke in wispy clouds, drifting high in the summer sky.

# CHANGING FORMATIONS

When painting landscapes outdoors, be prepared to make alterations to your sketch as you go along because cloud formations can change rapidly.

Try to record the light and shadow and the color tones. Simplify the cloud shapes as much as possible, and use artistic license to change any details.

Be sensitive to the way clouds work with and reflect the contours of the landscape.

# PAINTING SUNSETS

Create a glorious interplay of rich colors as they mingle wet into wet on your paper.

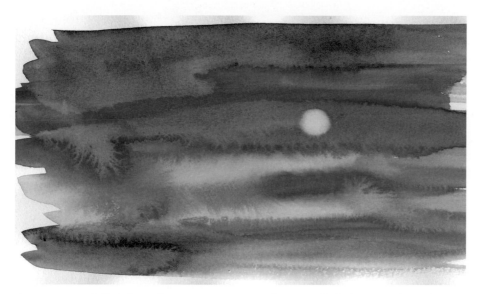

A sunset is difficult to draw, so just pencil in the shapes of the landscape.

Wet the entire sky with clear water. Now brush mixtures of sunset colors onto the surface in long, slow strokes, tilting the drawing board up so the colors can run down slightly. Use the edge of your sponge to blot out the area of the sun. When dry, paint in foreground details.

## Helpful Hint
To make fine branches, paint large ones in very watery strokes and use a straw to blow paint—carefully—in different directions.

# USING SALT

Salt is useful for creating a number of natural textures, such as snow and ice.

A few crystals of rock salt—not fine table salt—sprinkled onto wet paint creates a speckled effect.

## *Helpful Hint*

Don't be tempted to sprinkle on too much salt in one area—it will clump and you will not get the delicate, natural effect you are seeking.

The salt absorbs the moisture in the paint, leaving light marks that suggest crystals, ice, and snow. If the crystals are close together, they will form a mottled shape resembling weathered rock.

**1** Sprinkle the salt just as the shine in your wash goes dull. You have about 30 seconds to do it. If you put the salt on too soon it will just dissolve and leave strange marks. If you apply it too late then nothing will happen.

**2** The effect takes approximately 15 seconds to start working. Brush off any remaining salt when the paper is dry.

# USING MASKING FLUID

The transparent nature of watercolor makes it difficult to paint light areas over a dark background. In many cases, masking fluid is the answer.

Masking fluid is an adhesive rubber solution, available from art shops, that forms a resist when color is painted over the top of it. It can be easily applied with a brush or stick before or after a layer of paint is laid down. Then, when the paint is completely dry, the masking fluid can be rubbed off with your fingertip to reveal white paper or the layer of paint beneath. This method is much quicker than having to paint around intricate, detailed shapes.

**1** Masking fluid was applied first over the swirling shapes of the background grate, then to make complex markings on the lightly washed butterfly.

**2** As the background pattern is built up, and the butterfly is washed over with black, you can see the dramatic effects of the masking fluid.

Masking fluid has many uses, from the creation of intricate details, as here, to the protection of highlighted areas in landscape painting.

An effect similar to masking fluid can be achieved using wax, a crayon, or even a candle to resist the paint. Here, a crayon design shows through a watercolor wash.

# DARK BACKGROUNDS

A recessive background is handy when you wish your composition to emphasize the contrast between dominant light objects against a dark background.

With this painting, palely glowing flowers have been thrown forward by the darkly lit background wash. The terms "positive" and "negative" space are used to describe this balance, between the dominant light shapes (positive space) and the recessive dark background (negative space) that falls between them.

Because the main shapes are large enough, they can be painted first, with the simple dark background painted in later.

**1** First paint your main images. Here, the wet-into-wet technique was used.

**2** When the main image is dry, carefully paint in the darker background tones. It isn't necessary to bring the background color right up to the main image—don't be afraid to leave some white bits.

## Helpful Hint

If you have left too much white space around the images, it can be filled in simply by smudging the paint with a final wash of clear water.

With the loose wet-into-wet technique, it is interesting to see how color settles and runs together in certain places, creating natural-looking lighter and darker areas.

# SIMPLE BACKGROUNDS

When foreground objects are complex or dramatic, a loose background will create an effective contrast.

**1** After the composition has been sketched out and a few details added, the background can be painted before the main shapes are completed.

Paint the background wet into wet, using different combinations of recessive colors. Add water droplets in some areas to create watermarks and a loose effect. You may wish to use masking fluid to protect some of the petals.

**2** Now that the background is established, add faint washes to the petals, taking care not to wet and blur the background. Build up flower colors, painting wet into wet and wet on dry.

Add details and finishing touches to contrast with the plain background.

You can also see that each color was tested around the edge of the painting, making a delightfully decorative "self" border.

# BUILDINGS AND PERSPECTIVE

Painting buildings is a good way to familiarize yourself
with the principles of perspective.

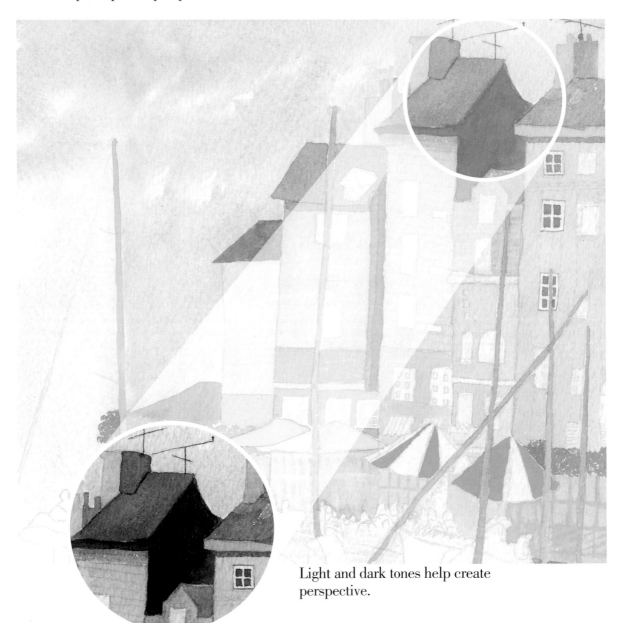

Light and dark tones help create
perspective.

In the detail of the painting at left, you will notice that the tones—light and dark areas—on the faces of the buildings help to define their planes and make the structures look three-dimensional. This painting is an example of two-point perspective, in which two angled faces of a building are seen at one time.

To help you judge the angles of the planes, you need to visualize lines of perspective receding to an imaginary vanishing point on the horizon.

## Two-point perspective

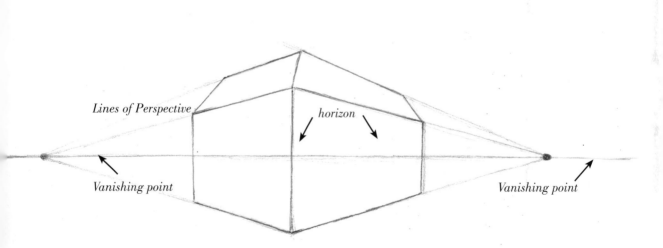

Lines of Perspective

horizon

Vanishing point

Vanishing point

One-point perspective is a simpler form of perspective, in which only one face of a building—or any other structure—is angled away from the viewer. This will allow you to concentrate on the relative size of objects in your painting.

## One-point perspective

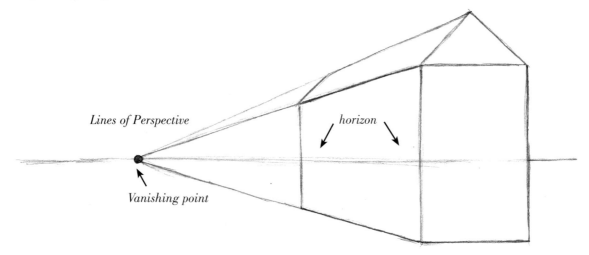

*Lines of Perspective*

*horizon*

*Vanishing point*

## *Helpful Hint*

1. On your sketch, use a ruler to draw in faint lines of perspective. Your vanishing point may fall outside your actual composition.
2. Perspective involves geometry, but even if you do not understand the principles fully, most people see and use perspective naturally.

Here the lines of perspective help you gauge not only the angles of the roof and the sidewalk but also the diminished size of objects in the distance.

See how these lines have helped the artist make the figure in the background the "same" height as the figures in the middle and foreground: you can tell this is so because their heads are all level with the same line of perspective. The trees are treated in a similar manner.

Even when the lines are erased in the finished painting, the viewer will intuitively see the relationship in size between the near and distant objects.

# REFLECTIVE SURFACES

Depicting a light-reflecting bottle is all
about painting technique, but first you must
get your drawing right.

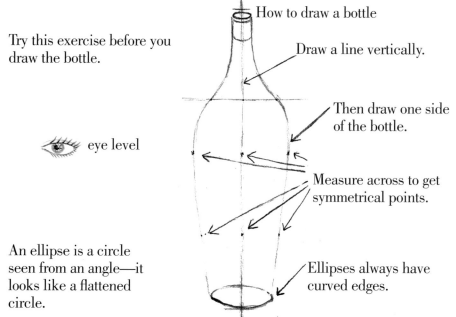

Try this exercise before you
draw the bottle.

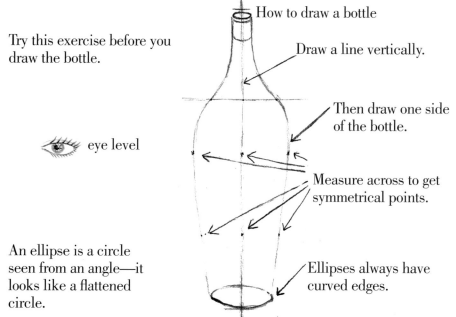 eye level

An ellipse is a circle
seen from an angle—it
looks like a flattened
circle.

How to draw a bottle

Draw a line vertically.

Then draw one side
of the bottle.

Measure across to get
symmetrical points.

Ellipses always have
curved edges.

# BOTTLES AND GLASSES

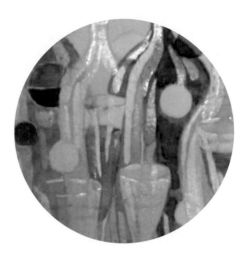

**1** Make a sketch, breaking each object down to its simplest form to enhance the eventual play of light on its surface.

**2** If there are any areas you wish to keep pure white, then use masking fluid to protect them. Place a very pale wash in each section. Remember to leave some areas white if you are not using masking fluid.

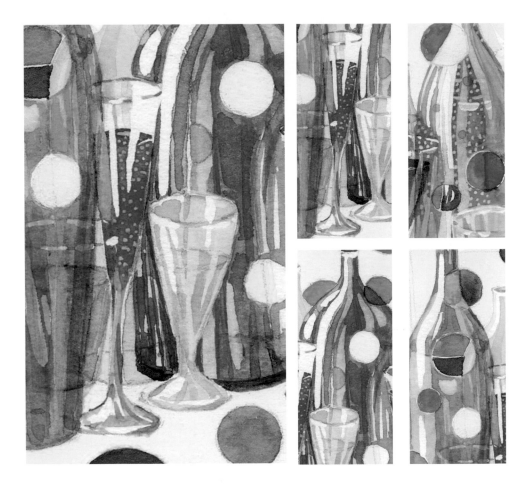

**3** Now gradually build up the layers of tone, leaving some sections of the underwashes visible.

Use a combination of wet-into-wet and wet-on-dry techniques in creating layers.

**4** Build up details and highlights, painting wet on dry.

Continue molding form, enriching colors, and adding bubbles.

**5** Make sure your white and lightly colored highlights are applied in long, continuous strokes that follow the contour of the bottles and mimic light reflecting off their surface.

*Helpful Hint*
You can use a hair dryer to speed up drying time when applying wet-on-dry layers of color. Set it at medium and hold it back from the paper.

# FIGURES AND FACES

The human form is easier to portray once you understand some basic principles about its shape.

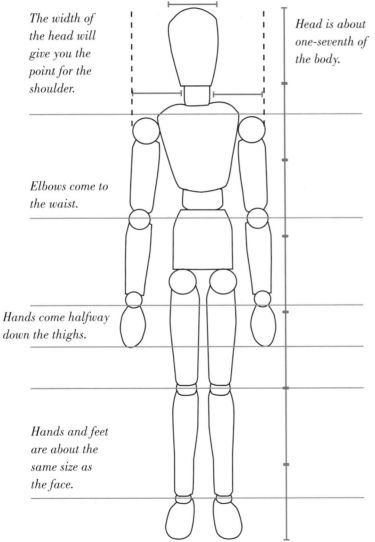

*The width of the head will give you the point for the shoulder.*

*Head is about one-seventh of the body.*

*Elbows come to the waist.*

*Hands come halfway down the thighs.*

*Hands and feet are about the same size as the face.*

Figures and faces follow certain proportional rules— Leonardo da Vinci did a lot of research into the anatomy of the figure and established some useful guidelines for artists.

The adult body and face sketched here show only aproximate proportions, but they will help you on your way to depicting lifelike form and movement.

To draw faces, you could work from a photo—especially if you want to capture an expression—or ask a friend to sit for you.

It is very hard to get a likeness, and it takes artists many years to master this skill, so just try your best and don't worry. If you capture a likeness in any area of the face, then you should feel very pleased with yourself.

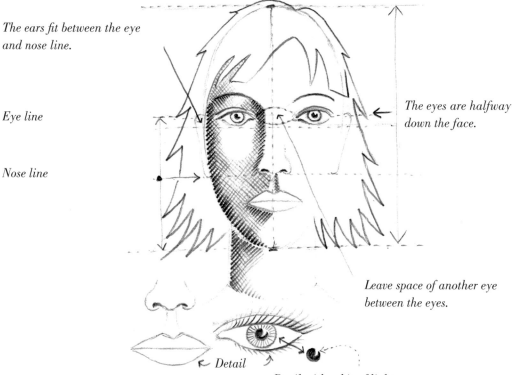

*The ears fit between the eye and nose line.*

*Eye line*

*Nose line*

*The eyes are halfway down the face.*

*Leave space of another eye between the eyes.*

*↙ Detail ↗*

*Pupil with a bit of light*

# LIFELIKE PORTRAIT

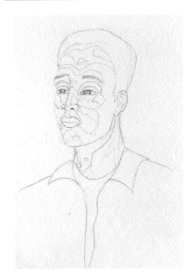

**1** First make your sketch, paying special attention to distinctive features and head shape, and delineating areas of light and shade in the contours of the face and neck.

**2** Paint in the features, aiming for a likeness, and begin building up very pale washes to get the contours right.

**3** Continue adding detail and building up light and dark tones.

Although the face itself should be the focal point, clothing worked loosely wet into wet, finely textured hair, and a decorative framing effect can complement the face and give clues to the subject's personality.

## *Helpful Hint*

If you cannot complete your portrait in one session, take a color photo to help you work up from your sketch later on.

# LESSONS

# LESSON 1: APRICOT TEA

## TRY THIS

*To prevent your cup and apricots from floating, add shadows of violet and cerulean to anchor them. Make sure shadows fall away from your imagined light source.*

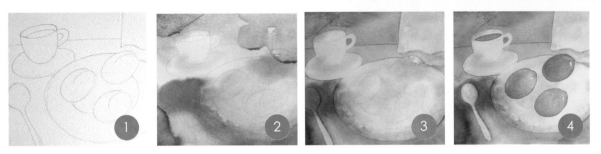

This still life is a good way to have fun with watercolor. You'll like the way the colors run into each other on the page.

**Step 1:** Make a light pencil drawing with your 3B pencil. Let some of the objects sit at funny angles.

**Step 2:** With your brush, flood the paper with clear water and let it evaporate for a few minutes. Using a selection of all your colors, drop in areas of paint, allowing them to mix on the paper. Don't worry if it looks a bit blobby—it's only a background. Allow to dry completely before continuing.

**Step 3:** For the background and tabletop, paint thin washes of color behind the cup, saucer, plate, and spoon. Use blues for the wall, and reds and yellows for the table. Note that you are making negative shapes here—the objects are created by leaving gaps in the background colors and not by painting them directly.

**Step 4:** Paint the apricots with a thin wash of yellow. As they are drying, flood in a brushload of vermilion. Paint the tea with a mix of sap green and vermilion, and a cerulean wash down the side of the spoon.

**Step 5:** Use white mixed with a little cerulean on a clean brush and paint the curtain — make a pattern by leaving negative areas (as in step 3). Paint blue lines on the china edges and red ones on the table-top — turn your paper as you work so you drag the brush toward you.

# LESSON 2:
# HARBOR BOATS

## TRY THIS

*When building up washes, make sure to let white areas in the walls, windows, boats, and water show through. This makes it look as if light is reflecting on the scene.*

This picture may look a little challenging — but it's really very easy to do if you experiment with colors and keep things simple.

**Step 1:** Sketch in the basic shapes with a pencil. Contrast the rounded shape of the boats with the straight sides of buildings and poles.

**Step 2:** Mix and lay on thin washes. The sky is a very watery mix of prussian blue with touch of vermilion. Trees are sap green with a dot of vermilion. Water is prussian blue darkened with vermilion. Paint sky and water on damp paper, trees on dry.

**Step 3:** On dry paper, paint on dull colors for buildings—experiment with very watery mixes of prussian blue and vermilion to get grays and browns. Paint boats in brighter colors, adding shadows as shown for greater depth.

**Step 4:** Continue with washes on buildings, keeping them light but solid looking. Build up

foliage on the trees, and make greens more intense by adding vermilion on the near tree.

**Step 5:** With a slightly darker blue mix, wash around bottom of boats. When your painting is dry, use a black fine liner to put in lines for poles and the strings on boats. Keep it simple to catch the freshness of a day on the water.

# LESSON 3: TULIP TIME

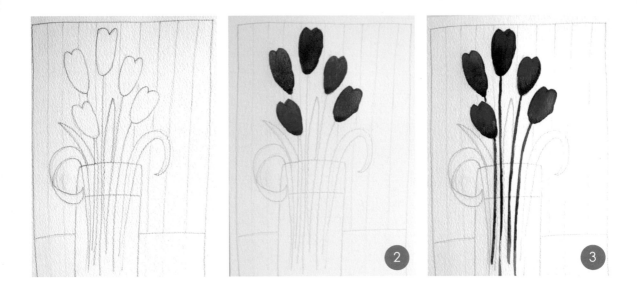

This is a good composition because its tall shape suits the tulips and vase. Trim your paper to fit.

**Step 1:** Make an outline sketch in pencil. It looks good to draw a frame to fit the drawing into.

**Step 2:** Using vermilion on its own, and mixed with your blues, paint flowers using a different combination for each. Start with one color, then while it is wet, add another at the base, and let them run together.

**Step 3:** Clean your brush and load with sap green. Touch the base and drag down to paint the stem of each wet flower. Let the colors run together.

**Step 4:** Let your painting dry. Then, in sap green, add thin lines to the background, and paint in leaves. Make a thin wash of green and vermilion for either side of vase. Add a touch of cerulean to the vermilion at the top and let the colors run together. When dry, run a pale wash over the whole vase.

## TRY THIS

*For painting wet-into-wet, steps 2, 4, and 5, try tilting the paper as the colors run and bleed into each other. This will give you some interesting, free effects.*

**Step 5:** With a watery brush of cerulean blue, define the water in the vase. Let your brush pick up some green from the stems to give a watery feel. Leave some clear areas. Add a few flicks of cerulean. When dry, add the finishing touches to your painting. Make a wash of cerulean, vermilion, and prussian blue and, with the tip of your brush, draw along the stems in the vase. Then with the whole brush, add a shadow along the side of each of the tulips.

# LESSON 4:
# SUMMER FIELD

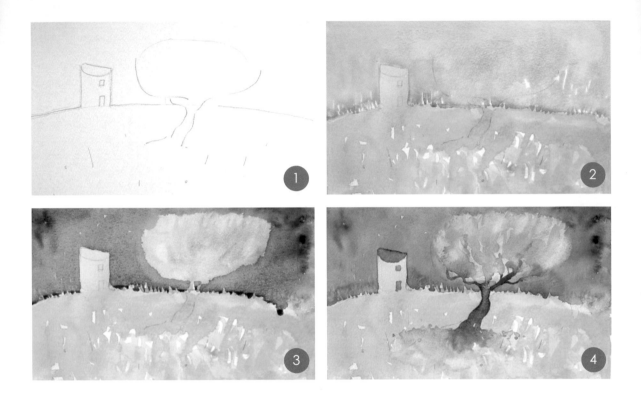

This sunny field with its olive tree and little mill was painted in Greece. Remember to take your watercolors on vacation with you this year.

**Step 1:** Make a light pencil sketch without showing any detail.

**Step 2:** With a mix of yellow and vermilion, wash the field and mill. While this is wet, mix sap green and cerulean, and cover the sky and olive tree. Leave areas of paper showing and let the paint run. Add touches of yellow where the field meets the sky.

**Step 3:** Use a darker mix of cerulean and sap green, and some pure cerulean, to make the sky darker around the tree. Use very dark color at the line above the field. Allow colors to mix on the paper and flick up some yellow grass with your brush.

**Step 4:** With a dark mix of cerulean and sap green, make light strokes in the tree for leaves. While still wet, mix vermilion and prussian with a bit of cerulean and use for branches and the trunk. As the trunk reaches the ground, add cerulean and draw into a shadow. With same color, paint the door and windows. Mix vermilion and lemon for the roof.

## TRY THIS

*Don't worry about letting pencil lines show through. They add interest and surprise the viewer.*

**Step 5:** When the painting is dry, add leaves to the olive tree using the brush tip with a mix of cerulean and sap green. Add strokes of yellow mixed with vermilion to the field to add interest to grass — make them large in the foreground and smaller in the background to help with perspective. Use pure vermilion and add poppies with one touch of your brush. With a warm blue wash, fill in white gaps in the field. With a red wash, draw more grasses and stems. Flick on strong colors with your brush to create clusters of wildflowers.

5

# LESSON 5:
# AT THE SEASIDE

## HELPFUL HINT

*Watercolor can be a very rewarding paint medium. Experiment with as many styles as possible until you find the one that suits you best.*

Look carefully at the colors used in this painting and see if you can achieve the same watery effects.

**Step 1:** With a pencil, sketch in the main shapes in the composition.

**Step 2:** Dampen your paper. Mix different blues and make wet-into-wet washes for the sea and sky. Add a sandy color for the beach, and shades of green to the cliff. Dab areas with tissue to dry off very wet areas and to lighten tints.

**Step 3:** Leave to dry, then paint the figure and its reflection in watery vermilion and prussian, letting the colors blend. Dampen the water area and add more blues. Add a blue wash to the cliff to give it shape.

**Step 4:** Now add more color and detail to the sand and rocks, using the same range of colors as before. Paint the flag in vermilion and blue.

**Step 5:** Use pure white for bubbles of foam — let them bleed into the surrounding colors. Deepen the color of the water behind the flag with a little more blue. Make small refinements but keep it simple. You can even use pastels on completely dry paper to add a little extra color to the figure, flag, sand, and water.

# LESSON 6: STILL LIFE

## HELPFUL HINT

*When you have learned and mastered the basics of watercolor painting, develop an adventurous nature. Be prepared to throw caution to the wind and experiment with the medium; you could be surprised at the results.*

Just as styles of handwriting vary from one person to another, so do styles of painting. In this still life demonstration a looser technique for painting with watercolors is used. Instead of sitting down to paint, try standing up. Standing encourages a looser approach and dramatically reduces the temptation to include fiddly detail.

**Step 1:** The group was set up and drawn out using a triangular composition. The light comes from a window on the right of the picture.

**Step 2:** Paint in the light and medium tones with a ½" (13 mm) flat wash brush and a No. 10 round brush.

**Step 3:** Add the darker tones with the point of a No. 10 round brush.

**Step 4:** Using a No. 6 round brush the key dark details to the wine bottle, glass, pineapple and lines of the check tablecloth.